Philemon & Titus

I0177026

GARY R. SMALL

Philemon & Titus
Copyright © 2023 by Gary R. Small

Scriptures taken from the Holy Bible, New International Version®, NIV®. Copyright © 1973, 1978, 1984, 2011 by Biblica, Inc.™ Used by permission of Zondervan. All rights reserved worldwide. www.zondervan.com The "NIV" and "New International Version" are trademarks registered in the United States Patent and Trademark Office by Biblica, Inc.™ Scripture quoted by permission. Quotations designated (NET) are from the NET Bible® copyright ©1996, 2019 by Biblical Studies Press, L.L.C. https://netbible.com All rights reserved. Scripture quotations are from the ESV® Bible (The Holy Bible, English Standard Version®), copyright © 2001 by Crossway, a publishing ministry of Good News Publishers. Used by permission. All rights reserved. The ESV text may not be quoted in any publication made available to the public by a Creative Commons license. The ESV may not be translated in whole or in part into any other language. Scripture quotations marked (AMPCE) are taken from the Amplified Bible, Copyright © 1954, 1958, 1962, 1964, 1965, 1987 by The Lockman Foundation. Used by permission. • Scripture quotations marked MSG are taken from The Message, copyright © 1993, 2002, 2018 by Eugene H. Peterson. Used by permission of NavPress. All rights reserved. Represented by Tyndale House Publishers.

Print ISBN: 978-1-4866-2400-3
eBook ISBN: 978-1-4866-2401-0

Word Alive Press
119 De Baets Street, Winnipeg, MB R2J 3R9
www.wordalivepress.ca

WORD ALIVE
—P R E S S—

Cataloguing in Publication may be obtained through Library and Archives Canada

Contents

Series Introduction

Keep this Book of the Law always on your lips; meditate on it day and night, so that you may be careful to do everything written in it. Then you will be prosperous and successful. (Joshua 1:8)

The word meditate and its derivatives occur eighteen times in the Bible. Of these, eight pertain to meditating on the Scriptures. Through these verses, we are encouraged to hold God's word in our hearts so that we might profit from His wisdom and be blessed by a closer relationship with Him (Psalm 119:1–3).

The secular world has also proposed the concept of taking a thoughtful approach to life and uses the word mindfulness to describe a contemplative lifestyle.

Mindfulness has been defined as "the awareness that arises through paying attention in the present moment, on purpose, nonjudgmentally."[1] Other terms have been applied to this intentional approach, such as *to internalize, to meditate on*, or *to process*. It is what we as Christians do when we carefully consider the Bible.

1 Judson Brewer, *Unwinding Anxiety* (New York, NY: Avery, 2021), 71. Quoting Jon Kabat-Zinn.

The trouble is that we often don't have time to study in this manner. Instead we find ourselves snatching moments in our busy lives to read, internalize, and digest passages from our daily reading of the Bible. By squeezing these most important moments of the day into the least number of minutes, we don't make time for the mindfulness required to truly digest God's word.

Another mistake we often fall into is having too high expectations of ourselves. We lean into weighty commentaries or topical novels on life-changing subjects and once again find that we don't have the sufficient time or headspace to do justice to the meaty subjects therein.

We previously referred to this problem as having too much pace and not sufficient peace to make sense of God's word. It is the challenge that led to the production of this series of books, which are designed to help lift a word from His word and make it poignant.

How we choose to use the selected word for each chapter will be different for each reader. Each chapter is designed to provoke mindful thought on a biblical passage. We have also provided three applications at the end of each chapter to stimulate further reflection.

It is hoped that the chosen word from each passage will be recalled throughout the day when we find moments of stillness or thought, so we can pay attention, on purpose, nonjudgmentally.

These books can be used by individuals. They may also find use in group settings to provoke further discussion on a sermon series or in small group Bible study.

It is hoped that the books will be used as a spiritual tool to reinvigorate your Bible reading and provide impetus to make a life change as a Christian.

The concept is simple, one which by no means seeks to detract from the value of in-depth Bible study. There is still a place for this when time allows and further reading references are provided. We have taken care to tread a middle road theologically and avoid weighty arguments on some finer points of hermeneutics, although some of these can be found within the referenced material.

We sincerely hope that *A Word from His Word* will not only lift selected words from the pages of Scripture but also provide a lift to your Bible reading and spiritual life.

Much has been made by the secular world of the benefits of mindfulness. I suspect this discipline is not new, although it has perhaps been lost in our striving for scientific purpose. Yet there is, in this series, an opportunity to rediscover the usefulness of intentional meditation on God's word (Psalm 1:1–2).

Foreword

Choosing a book that will become one's companion for a few weeks may be a small task, but it's not an insignificant one. No one wants to fritter away precious time with a book that doesn't deliver on its promises or their expectations. We want to be stirred by what we read. We want our thirst for new thoughts and new writing to be quenched.

We read, yearning for inspiration, enthused by the material we expect to cover, and excited to start afresh with the hope of gaining insight into our own hearts. As with daybreak, we embark upon a new project like reading this edition of *A Word from His Word*, looking for sunlight, imagining warmth, and expecting growth.

Philemon and Titus are seldom used as teaching material. I cannot think of many occasions when passages from either letter have been used as the basis for a sermon. They are not regulars for study in church house groups or Bible studies. They are underrated, a term borrowed from a description of Montepulciano grapes, which, just like Philemon and Titus, are also underappreciated.

Far from being bland, both of these letters from Paul are full of substance. Both have distinctive flavours. Philemon is a piece of personal correspondence from midway through Paul's ministry life, whereas Titus is pastoral letter from the end of Paul's life. Neither is short on punch and together they provide lessons which can be long savoured.

This book may be used as a standalone resource. Each chapter includes a Bible reading with a brief commentary. In the commentary, the focus is on a word or phrase from the scripture passage, with the goal of promoting further thought, prayer, and application on the focus word. One chapter may be read per day, or per week, and it may lend itself to being read alone or shared in a group setting.

As with other books from this series, *Philemon & Titus* is meant to create some of those precious moments that we experience like the dawn of a new day. These are moments we can spend with God and in our thoughts, praying with the Father.

Just as the rich taste of Montepulciano D'Abruzzo wine catches some off-guard, I hope this study into these less familiar letters will provide you with rich, quality time with God. Such quiet moments with Him are always sought after once a new day dawns, but like a great wine, or a great book, they are hard to come by.

Introduction

PHILEMON

The traditional interpretation of this short letter is that it was written by Paul and Timothy to Philemon, his household, and the Colossian church that met in Philemon's house.

Philemon was thought to have been a prominent figure in the early Colossian church. Apphia may have been his wife and Archippus his son. The letter was penned regarding a crisis situation concerning a runaway slave from Philemon's household. The slave, called Onesimus, had come into the sphere of Paul, had converted to Christianity, and was now returning home.

The letter is thought to have been written from Rome, where Paul was under house arrest, around the same time as the letter to the Colossians in AD 60. Some have argued that the letter was written from Ephesus, since it is more geographically plausible for Onesimus to have escaped to Ephesus (100 miles from Colossae) than Rome (1,300 miles away). Those who advocate Rome, however, have highlighted that city's advantages to runaway slaves, since it was easier to become hidden amidst its large population.

As to how Onesimus became a Christian or how he fell in with Paul, the letter doesn't provide further details, although both events are incredulous in themselves.

For the casual observer, the letter was cause for celebration. A new Christian had come to faith, a new co-worker for Paul had been found, and the reconciliation between a former master and his runaway slave was in the cards.

Celebration was also due to mark the growing trust and mutual respect between Philemon and Paul. Paul had been effusive in his praise of the Colossians and remained anxious to visit these people and their church. It's easy to imagine Paul's joy in anticipating a visit to a Christian community that had arisen without his own direct involvement and in whom Christ's message seemed to be maturing with oak-like vigour and resolve.

Hidden not too far beneath the initial greetings and diplomacy of the letter, however, are far weightier matters.

A potentially divisive church debate was brewing as to how Philemon would deal with his runaway slave. If he were too weak, he might incur the disapproval of the Christian society with whom he lived and worked. Alternatively, voices in the newly founded church might have been espousing mercy and forgiveness for Onesimus, perhaps using many of the arguments Paul himself poses throughout the letter. If Philemon were too harsh, his standing amongst these people would have suffered.

Philemon was also under pressure from secular quarters to be seen to be acting appropriately. He apparently had accumulated some wealth, since he had spare rooms in his house, and the advice of his well-to-do friends when it came to punishing Onesimus might have run contrary to the grace expected by Paul. Whether from the worldly perspective or that of the church, Philemon's honour was at stake. How he responded would have been carefully watched.

Paul himself was also under scrutiny. He wrote the letter under house arrest due to the civil disturbances that had accompanied his evangelism. Paul, in advocating for Onesimus, would have needed to be careful not to test the ire of the Rome authorities. If he were seen to be condoning the lax treatment of runaway slaves, this might be used as evidence of his tendency to promote civil unrest. Secular society certainly would have disapproved of Paul writing on behalf of a slave, let alone suggesting that Onesimus might be treated a brother to his former master. Rather than take responsibility for writing, Paul might have been wise to mind his own business. He didn't need to court any further legal trouble that might have reduced his chances of release. Onesimus was, after all, a slave and of no value in the world's eyes. Paul would have been justified, from a legal perspective, to ignore Onesimus's plight.

Paul might have also suffered criticism from some in the church. His initial harbouring of the slave might have caused divisions. Why bring this extra pressure on their movement at a time when persecution was becoming widespread? Others in the church, sympathetic to Onesimus, might have been critical of Paul's insistence that Onesimus return, which could have led him to face the death penalty.

For Paul, like Philemon, there was integrity and honour at stake as they worked through this crisis.

Onesimus's integrity was also being tested. He might have been forgiven for not being eager to return home, since his future with Philemon would have been uncertain at best. He had managed to make it as far as Rome and for all intents and purposes had become a free man. He had been lost in the crowds of the city and put his past behind him. From the world's perspective he would have been well advised to keep his head down, work as a free man, and not look back.

Somewhere in this story, however, he miraculously came to faith, and at the time of Paul's writing Onesimus was being asked to demonstrate tremendous commitment to this new faith. He was being asked to forgo worldly wisdom and return to his previous master.

For each of our main characters—Paul, Onesimus, and Philemon—their honour was tested. Their self-respect and integrity as Christians were under the microscope.

This letter to Philemon is far from being an irrelevant piece of historical correspondence. Rather, it vividly captures a crisis in the early church, speaking to sensitive issues of betrayal, penitence, changed lives, and second chances. It touches on the issues of slavery, which is still a raw and sensitive topic. And at its heart, as we have noted, the letter highlights the root of man's motives. From where would they seek honour? Would it be sought from secular wisdom or from God?

There is so much we can learn from the letter to Philemon. Whether we take a step back and reflect on Paul's diplomacy, marvel at the courage of Onesimus to return, or consider how Philemon would have reacted, each angle is worthy of our time and study.

As we begin this edition of *A Word from His Word*, take a moment to reflect on this central theme: from where do we seek our honour, and do we seek the approval of men or of God?

> Another saying of Jesus, and a most disturbing one, was put in the form of a question, "How can ye believe, which receive honour one of another, and seek not the honour that cometh from God alone?" (KJV John 5:44). If I understand this correctly Christ taught here the alarming doctrine that the desire for honor among men made belief impossible.[2]

---

2 A.W. Tozer, *The Pursuit of God* (Bloomington, MN: Baker House, 2014), 97.

Grace and Peace

PHILEMON 1–3

Paul, a prisoner of Christ Jesus, and Timothy our brother,

To Philemon our dear friend and fellow worker—[2] also to Apphia our sister and Archippus our fellow soldier—and to the church that meets in your home: [3] Grace and peace to you from God our Father and the Lord Jesus Christ.

A crisis is about to unfold in a marriage, a household, and a church. The return of a runaway slave would create uncertainty on multiple levels. Would Apphia, traditionally considered to be Philemon's wife, be supportive of Philemon whatever his decision regarding Onesimus? What would the other servants of the household think of Onesimus's return? And how would their house church react?

Uncertainty breeds anxiety and can lead to a lack of clarity of thought.

The best decisions often aren't made with an anxious mind. Anxiety may lead to fear, the fear of physical reprisals or the fear of emotional or psychological abuse, and fear can lead to panic, which can be the worst possible reaction when uncertainty looms.

Paul and Timothy wisely grounded all this uncertainty in two core values of Christianity: grace and peace. Philemon 3 is far from being a formulaic beginning to a standard letter; there is an appeal here for the letter's recipients to centre their emotions so they can reflect on its contents with less uncertainty, anxiety, fear, and panic.

Grace is more that simple mercy, and it was typified so perfectly in the actions of Christ on the cross. In the midst of brutality, He offered this amazing gift to those who believed in His name. We did not deserve his mercy, we did not warrant his forgiveness, and we were not worthy to untie His sandals, yet in spite of all this He offered us the chance to be adopted into His family to become a child of His Father, to stand forgiven, accepted, and loved.

Paul and Timothy reminded their readers that it is the grace of Christ that binds them together both as a church and as fellow Christians.

Grace is a great leveller. It dispels any illusion that we are made worthy on the basis of our own self-righteousness. For the house of Philemon, they may have felt justified as individuals, or even as a corporate body. The mention of grace dismisses this misconception and reminded them, and us, that without Christ's love we have done nothing to merit praise from God or dispel anxiety. Without grace, we can have no peace.

The mention of peace in the same breath of grace reminded the readers of this letter of the link between these two states. We receive grace and we feel peace. Peace of mind is a rare gift, for it dispels anxiety, fear, and panic both for immediate concerns and future uncertainties.

Paul is keen that before he goes on to discuss the main issues before them, the group must be settled, of calm and sound mind, and ready to address the moral dilemmas that face them.

APPLICATION: GRACE AND PEACE

- Spend a moment reflecting on the grace of Christ that allows us to access Him and His Father with such amazing familiarity. Perhaps also let this lead you into the Lord's prayer.
- Like the recipients of this letter, you may be facing anxiety and uncertainty. Take a moment to read John 14:27 and bless Jesus for giving His peace constantly, without interruption, and without expectation.
- If you are in the midst of crises, consider the approach of Paul and Timothy: His grace and peace will be needed if you are to make strong decisions with a sound mind.

The ultimate measure of a man is not where he stands in moments of comfort and convenience, but where he stands at times of challenge and controversy. The true neighbor will risk his position, his prestige, and even his life for the welfare of others. In dangerous valleys and hazardous pathways, he will lift some bruised and beaten brother to a higher and more noble life.[3]

—Martin Luther King, Jr.

---

3 Martin Luther King, Jr., *The Words of Martin Luther King, Jr* (New York, NY: Newmarket Press, 1987), 9.

Deepening Your Understanding
PHILEMON 4–7

I always thank my God as I remember you in my prayers, [5] because I hear about your love for all his holy people and your faith in the Lord Jesus. [6] I pray that your partnership with us in the faith may be effective in deepening your understanding of every good thing we share for the sake of Christ. [7] Your love has given me great joy and encouragement, because you, brother, have refreshed the hearts of the Lord's people.

Through these verses, Paul and Timothy continue in diplomatic prayer, laying the groundwork for their appeal to Philemon, his household, and the Church. Were we less familiar with their characters, we might suspect that Paul and Timothy were laying on the affability a little too thick to be genuine. However, we know that Paul often turned to intercessory prayer when it came to his fellow Christians; it was one of his spiritual disciplines (Romans 1:9, 1 Corinthians 1:4, Ephesians 1:16, Colossians 1:3).

Although Philemon 6 is ambiguous and its meaning in the New International Version is unclear, it is an important verse in the context of the letter. The "your" is singular and therefore must refer primarily to Philemon. Paul is calling Philemon to do something here, although exactly what that was left unsaid. But the intention of the verse is to indicate that Paul had expectations for Philemon's behaviour now that he shared a partnership with and other Christians.

The New English Translation translates the verse this way: *"I pray that the faith you share with us may deepen your understanding of every blessing that belongs to you in Christ"* (NET).

It is the middle portion of the verse that is difficult to grasp. What does Paul mean when he encourages Philemon to "deepen your understanding of every blessing"? This phrase, "deepen your understanding," speaks to increasing one's knowledge or perception. The Greek word used here for understanding is *epiginosko*, which is a compound word from *epi* (upon) and *ginosko* (to know experientially). Paul is inviting Philemon to deepen his heartfelt understanding.

That which Paul is calling on Philemon to understand is explained at the end of the verse by the term "every good thing". In Greek the term is simply "every good" - pantos agathou-; so the verse ends "every good that is in us through Christ". Agathou was usually employed to express good works or good deeds (see verse 14). This passage thus has tones that echo Ephesians 2:10: *"For we are God's handiwork, created in Christ Jesus to do good works, which God had prepared in advance for us to do."* It speaks of the ethically sound, morally upright works God has called each of us to do if we would listen to His guiding direction.

Ephesians 2:10 is one of those verses that enables us to trust our careers and lives to God, knowing that He has our direction

5

in mind and that, although it can sometimes seem otherwise, He is directing our paths provided that we listen to and obey His voice.

Paul is intimating to Philemon that there are good works laid out for him in God's plan for his life. Further, Paul indicates that we can access understanding and know these good works through fellowship with other Christians.

As readers of the letter, we know what crisis Paul is about to introduce into Philemon's life, so we perceive in this verse some advice and a plea for Philemon to invoke Christian fellowship to better understand the right, true, and moral path through his situation.

I suspect that Philemon 6 resonates with our own experiences of difficult times. God's will is often best understood when we discuss our problems and situations with trusted Christians, in whose company and advice we are reminded of the importance of our fellowship with one another and with Him. We are no longer alone in our crisis. Furthermore, we recall that He will provide a way out that will marry our conscience with His will so that His peace remains in our hearts.

Such paths are not always easy, and I expect that Philemon's decisions were difficult. His heavy burden would no doubt have threatened to bend him over. The blessing from following God's understanding, however, would have been like warm sun on Philemon's aching back, enabling him to straighten up, walk tall, and make it through this crisis.

APPLICATION: DEEPENING YOUR UNDERSTANDING

- Do you understand that God has a plan for your life and has prepared works for you to do?
- Thank God that no matter the crises you face, or difficulties that arise, God has prepared a response for you in advance. In fellowship with Him, and others, the answers to your crises can be understood.
- Take a moment to thank God for Philemon, for his witness in His household and His encouragement for the early church. Consider Philemon like folks you know in your own life and pray that in fellowship with other Christians they may understand the blessings they have in Christ.

Son

Therefore, although in Christ I could be bold and order you to do what you ought to do, [9] yet I prefer to appeal to you on the basis of love. It is as none other than Paul—an old man and now also a prisoner of Christ Jesus—[10] that I appeal to you for my son Onesimus, who became my son while I was in chains. [11] Formerly he was useless to you, but now he has become useful both to you and to me.

[12] I am sending him—who is my very heart—back to you.

Paul writes of the return of Onesimus, whose homecoming retains a flavour reminiscent of Jesus's parable about the prodigal son. The act of returning implies that one has repented; it's an acknowledgement that the decision to strike out in a particular direction was wrong. The chosen path was misguided. By returning, one is renewing their commitment to try again and walk a better path, a path more in line with the household.

Onesimus's return reflected his newfound Christian faith and the instruction of his father in the faith. His return wasn't just a figurative repentance and acknowledgment of wrongdoing; it was courageously symbolic, for a slave choosing to return home after fleeing was not something to be done lightly. The consequences may have been devastating, if not tragic.

In order to perceive the courage and faith of Onesimus, we should recognize the dangers he was walking into. His brave actions to travel back to Philemon demonstrated a strong belief that Christian love could stand apart from secular expectations. The Christian love he had learned about through the gospel had given him belief in the mercy, forgiveness, grace, and love that he would receive from Philemon.

Paul refers to Onesimus as his son. He is sending his "son" in the faith back to Philemon and the church in Colossae, to be subjected to their justice and mercy. No doubt Paul used this evocative term on purpose to stir compassion in the heart of the readers. It would not have been lost on them that they, too, were now children of a heavenly Father, adopted because of their faith in Christ.

Let us be reminded from these verses of our own adoption by God as His children. In its purest sense, there is something deeply poignant about being adopted as a child. The strength of bond between a child and parent is deeper and stronger than that of friendship. The bond is of higher quality, withstands greater challenges, and holds people up through life's difficulties. The parent-child relationship is a lifelong commitment to love, cherish, and respect one another.

Our life in Christ is to be lived in the context of such a relationship, as it was for Onesimus. Of course, our bond with Christ isn't merely for life; it is an eternal, everlasting relationship. This eternal nature adds further substance to our adoption, giving us even more reason to celebrate and be thankful for the lasting nature of this amazing gift.

These verses from the life story of Onesimus give us pause to reflect on the prodigal son story and of our own sonship experiences with our heavenly Father. We have all strode out on independent paths with rebellion in our hearts at some point, we have come to understand that there was a different route we should have taken, and then we returned to that route and began our journey home.

Our journeys are less of a return and more of a realignment, but emotionally I think we feel like we are returning home. Our return, however, does not fill our hearts with trepidation. In that sense, we are different from Onesimus. Our return has been paved by Christ, so we can be confident that we are returning to an accepting and gracious Father.

APPLICATION: SON

- Consider yourself as the returning prodigal son. Give thanks that you return to a gracious Father who is already preparing a feast for your homecoming.
- Pray for Onesimus-like courage to face obstacles when fear might be overwhelming. Thank God for the courage of Onesimus to believe in the goodness of those to whom he was returning.
- Thank God for spiritual parents like Paul who have guided your own faith when you were first adopted into God's family.

Brother in the Lord

PHILEMON 13-16

I would have liked to keep him with me so that he could take your place in helping me while I am in chains for the gospel. [14] But I did not want to do anything without your consent, so that any favor you do would not seem forced but would be voluntary. [15] Perhaps the reason he was separated from you for a little while was that you might have him back forever—[16] no longer as a slave, but better than a slave, as a dear brother. He is very dear to me but even dearer to you, both as a fellow man and as a brother in the Lord.

In our reflections on Paul's letter to Philemon, we have considered how Onesimus's return has similarities to the prodigal son parable (Luke 15:11–32). Our comparisons have drifted between Onesimus being the prodigal and Philemon being the father figure.

Today's passage sees Philemon take on a different role. Paul makes an appeal for Philemon to consider Onesimus as a brother in the Lord (Philemon 16). Commentators have suggested this was more than an emotional plea for kindness; rather, it represents Paul's suggestion that Onesimus should be set free.

Even for well-behaved, hard-working slaves, freedom was not easily obtained. If this was Paul's intent, it would have been an extraordinary request. To free a runaway slave who had returned would not have made common sense. It would have been without precedent, and legally it would have been frowned upon. Such an action could have tempted other slaves to run away. It could also have produced subversive behaviour that was contrary to the accepted social or cultural norms.

Although I would like to agree with those commentators who believe it was indeed Paul's wish for Onesimus to be freed, the emotional affect of Paul's appeal to brotherhood does not rest on this interpretation. In the appeal to brotherhood, one can perceive a petition for forgiveness, a plea for acceptance, and an overture for Philemon to move on from any bitterness he may have harboured following Onesimus's unexpected departure.

Earlier in the letter, Paul wrote that he held Philemon in high esteem, elevating him in his thoughts to that of his own brother (Philemon 7), because Philemon had refreshed the hearts of the Lord's people. Philemon by all accounts was an encourager of people, an optimist who lifted the spirits of those around him. He was a glass-half-full type, usually seeing the brighter side of life. In Philemon 16, Paul reminds Philemon of his earlier compliment by reusing the word brother and calls on Philemon to have a similarly generous heart and adopt Onesimus as a brother.

When we draw comparisons to the prodigal son story, we might perceive Philemon as the disenchanted elder brother, usually so dutiful and full of enthusiasm for his station in his father's house, yet the darker side of his personality comes out on the day of his brother's return. Rather than sharing the father's joy in the return of the prodigal, the brother displays anger, jealousy, resentment, and even hatred toward his younger brother (Luke 15:28–30).

My sense is that Paul, by using the term "brother in the Lord," is asking Philemon to put aside such natural responses. He is asking Philemon not to be a brother in the flesh, like the elder brother in the prodigal son story, and rather challenges him to reach into the depths of his heart, and that of Christ, to find the strength to forgive Onesimus. Whether forgiveness will entail the slave's freedom or his simple reintegration into the household is less important than the act itself.

Crises are not easy to navigate, and this was certainly true for Philemon and Onesimus, even as they both accepted Christ and sincerely walked in the light of His gospel. We have experienced our own crises and will experience more before we are called home. Should we find ourselves in Philemon's position, our challenge will be to behave more like a brother or sister in the Lord than the elder brother.

Paul would appeal to us not to be a brother in the flesh but a brother in Christ, less of a brother in the law and more of a brother in the Spirit.

APPLICATION: BROTHER IN THE LORD

- If you have a chance, read Luke 15:28–30. It is often easier to perceive the elder brother's sharpness than it is to consider your own. Reflect on how you have

13

dealt with, or are dealing with, a crisis. Ask God to give you more grace to be a brother or sister in Christ to those you are dealing with.

- Take a moment to pray for those you consider brothers or sister in the Lord. Give thanks for their example.
- Paul walked a fine line in his letter. He elevated Onesimus to the station of a brother and did not infringe on the rights of Philemon to decide what happened next. Pray for Paul-like wisdom when faced with crises, so that you may appeal to the best in others and not overstep your footing in relationships.

Refresh My Heart

PHILEMON 17–25

So if you consider me a partner, welcome him as you would welcome me. [18] If he has done you any wrong or owes you anything, charge it to me. [19] I, Paul, am writing this with my own hand. I will pay it back—not to mention that you owe me your very self. [20] I do wish, brother, that I may have some benefit from you in the Lord; refresh my heart in Christ. [21] Confident of your obedience, I write to you, knowing that you will do even more than I ask.

[22] And one thing more: Prepare a guest room for me, because I hope to be restored to you in answer to your prayers.

[23] Epaphras, my fellow prisoner in Christ Jesus, sends you greetings. [24] And so do Mark, Aristarchus, Demas and Luke, my fellow workers.

[25] The grace of the Lord Jesus Christ be with your spirit.

Paul ends his letter with his usual greetings and signature. He signs off on his appeal to Philemon, wishing for him to *"refresh my heart in Christ."* It is a wonderful prayer. It speaks to Philemon being able to inspire Paul, to lift him from his situation of house arrest in Rome into a position of joy.

Paul used the same phrase to describe Philemon in Philemon 7, in a sense encouraging him to be true to himself, true to the self that Philemon had become in the Lord.

This was perceptive of Paul, as it speaks to the understanding of who we have become in Christ. This is important, for the decisions we make in crises can leave us feeling disappointed with ourselves if we have compromised our new selves. Such disappointment can linger and ruminate so that our thoughts are unhelpful and distance us from God.

It is better to be consistent with the person God has called us to be and base our decisions on His guidance. The wisdom of decisions based on His wisdom will refresh the hearts of others and give us peace in our own hearts.

The word "refresh" was translated from the Greek *anapauson*, which speaks to being given rest, or being freed from sorrow. As Paul signs off on his personal note, he asks that Philemon be true to the nature Paul knows he has and accept Onesimus. If Philemon had the resources within him to do this, it would relieve Paul's anxiety and he would feel a huge relief.

When we consider our roles in crises, I suspect we would like to be considered individuals who refresh the hearts of others. I suspect that this is not always easy. It certainly would not have been easy for Philemon to do as Paul asked in relation to Onesimus. Yet if Philemon was true to his faith in Christ, the appropriate decision would have been plain: accept Onesimus, make him a freed man, and send him back to Paul.

It can be hoped that Philemon had the courage to follow up with Paul's hints and intimations.

In our dilemmas, may we remember the diplomacy of Paul as he sought to bring out the very best in Philemon. It seems that Paul was able to inspire honour and integrity within Onesimus, so we must hope that Philemon also lived up to Paul's expectations.

Perhaps this letter will give us the strength to draw upon Christ's wisdom to walk in line with His wishes and refresh the hearts of others.

APPLICATION: REFRESH MY HEART

- Thank God for those you know who refresh your heart to live a godly life.
- Consider how you can refresh the hearts of others.
- Take a moment to thank God for the roles of each of the characters in this letter: Paul, Onesimus, and Philemon. May their courage and integrity lead you to refresh your heart in Christ.

If I can help somebody as I pass along, if I can cheer somebody with a word or song, if I can show somebody he's traveling wrong, then my living will not be in vain. If I can do my duty as a Christian ought, if I can bring salvation to a world once wrought, if I can spread the

message as the master taught, then my living will not
be in vain.[4]

—Martin Luther King, Jr.

4 Martin Luther King, Jr., *The Autobiography of Martin Luther King, Jr.*, ed. Clayborne Carson (New York, NY: Intellectual Properties Management Inc., Grand Central Publishing), 366.

Reflections

PHILEMON

> Your love has given me great joy and encouragement, because you, brother, have refreshed the hearts of the Lord's people. (Philemon 7)

I found Philemon a surprisingly refreshing read. It is the third shortest book in the Bible by original word count and hence might be thought to be short on inspiration and lessons. Yet this letter from Paul and Timothy draws out the themes of dignity, honour, and integrity. These are challenging virtues, for it is not easy to align our behaviour in a fallen world to that which is expected by our heavenly Father.

We cannot see the future, and the consequences of our actions are not always discernible. What might seem wise can turn out to be painful in the short-term but rewarding in the long-term. I so wish for that long-term vision, to demonstrate greater trust to accept that God's wisdom is always the best wisdom.

In that regard, I found Philemon to be inspiring. I wish for Onesimus-like courage to face the uncertainties which can seem overwhelming. I hope for diplomacy and love, like Paul, to walk that thin line between being a guide versus being an authoritarian. In keeping with these thoughts, I hope to be a brother in Christ, like Philemon, and to avoid being like the elder brother from the parable of the prodigal son.

I have also enjoyed reading Martin Luther King, Jr.'s autobiography as a companion to Philemon. King demonstrated the type of dignity Paul asked for from Philemon. He mirrored the courage of Onesimus and did not allow the evil he confronted to turn him from the good deeds he had been called to do. King was deeply hurt by the tragedies that surrounded the protests against segregation, but he had a vision that enabled him to stay the course.

Paul's letter to Philemon has over the years been used as a platform to discuss Christian attitudes toward slavery. Sadly, the letter has been used to argue both sides of the debate. I hope that our reflections have helped to draw us away from such a focus. In elevating the letter to a piece of correspondence regarding honour, dignity, and Christian integrity, my intention is to highlight the reality that those character traits can have no place in slavery.

Given our reflections, it is disappointing that slavery and segregation persisted as long as they have. We are indebted to courageous individuals like Rosa Parks, King, and his associates for bringing such injustices to the attention of the world.

Throughout his short professional life, King refreshed the hearts of others. He has been an inspiration to many generations. An important component of his inspirational character was the integrity that was evident in his life. He admitted in his autobiography to making an intentional effort to ensure that he was consistent at home and in public so as to maintain an appropriate perspective on his life.[5] Evidence of this includes his use of biblical metaphors and Christian principles. He never shied away from relating his opinions to his Christian belief, and his speeches are full of biblical illustrations. He made it seem as if it should be natural for secular and Christian listeners to be familiar with such terms. And when times were difficult and the depravity of his opponents were at their worse, King drew on the deep well of the Holy Spirit to refresh his soul.

As we reflect on our own abilities to remain steadfast in the face of crises, we would do well to use the examples from the letter of Philemon and King himself. The difficulties we face in remaining true to our faith should not be underestimated or understated. Remaining dignified under pressure is not easy. Being consistent with Christian wisdom in the face of worldly influences is hard.

The letter to Philemon, while not giving precise instructions, provides an example of others who refreshed the hearts of believers by holding true to their faith in adversity. The well from which they drew so deeply has not run dry and remains available to us.

Having to live under the threat of death every day, sometimes I feel discouraged. Having to take so much abuse and criticism, sometimes from my own people, sometimes I feel discouraged. Having to go to bed so often frustrated with the chilly winds of adversity about to staffer me, sometimes I feel discouraged and feel my works in vain.

5 Ibid., 105.

But then the Holy Spirit revives my soul again. In Gilead, there is balm to make the wounded whole. If we will believe that, we will build a new Memphis. And bring about the day when every valley shall be exalted. Every mountain and hill will be made low. The rough places will be made plain, and the crooked places made straight. And the glory of the Lord shall be revealed, and all flesh shall see it together.[6]

—Martin Luther King, Jr.

---

6 Ibid., 354–355.

Introduction

TITUS

The pastoral letter to Titus was written later than AD 62, although a precise dating isn't possible. It seems to have come from a time late in Paul's ministry, or possibly after his death, for the church was beginning to develop a structure, suggesting that it was maturing as an organization. Paul's instruction for Titus to place elders in all the towns on Crete indicates that there was a need to develop a local hierarchy. This perhaps indicates a waning influence of the original apostles or the council in Jerusalem.

The book has also been difficult to date since there is no mention of Titus in Acts, nor of Paul visiting Crete on a ministry journey. He does briefly visit the island during his transfer into captivity in Rome around 59–60 AD. Recall that Paul had been arrested in Jerusalem, transferred to Caesarea, and remained there for two years. At that time, a change occurred in the local governor. The new appointee offered Paul the chance to return to Jerusalem to answer the charges against him, but Paul chose instead to appeal to Caesar. He was thereafter sent as a prisoner to Rome and remained there for at least two years.

It's not clear what happened next for Paul, as the book of Acts ends with him spending two years in Rome under house arrest. From the book of Titus and 1 and 2 Timothy, we might be led to believe that Paul was released and allowed to embark on a further missionary journey that directly or indirectly led him to Nicopolis on the west coast of Greece (Titus 3:12).

At some point after 62 AD, Paul appears to have been reimprisoned in Rome. In contrast to his initial interment under house arrest, his final captivity was spent in a cold place that required him to wear a cloak. One could postulate that during this time he languished in a dungeon, perhaps the notorious Mamertine prison. Paul was not optimistic about being released from his second captivity (2 Timothy 4).

By this time, Titus had seemingly left Crete and gone to Dalmatia, in modern-day Croatia (2 Timothy 4:9). If Paul was the author, the letter to Titus must have been written between Paul's first and second interments.

Some have questioned the letter's authenticity as a genuine Pauline work, since the letter seems to have been written at a date beyond Paul's ministry, to a church he did not visit in Acts, and only a third of the words used are similar to more secure Pauline works.

However, most do agree that the thrust of the text, the foundation of the arguments, and the overall ethos of the letter are Pauline in nature. Furthermore, the personal content of the letter suggests a close relationship between the author and recipient, as existed between Paul and Titus.

For the purposes of our devotions, we will refer to Paul as the author.

The church in Crete may have been founded by Cretans who were present at the first Pentecost (Acts 2:11). It seems unlikely that the island was evangelized by Paul, for there is no mention of this in Acts. Paul left Titus behind after their visit to *"put in order what was left unfinished and appoint elders in every town"* (Titus 1:5). This indicates that Paul did visit Crete, but by then there were multiple churches on the island that required organization.

Paul describes Titus as his true son (Titus 1:4), suggesting that Titus was a disciple of the apostle and most likely had been converted to Christianity through Paul's witness. Paul had travelled with Titus to Jerusalem where Titus was used as an example of the purity of faith that could exist in Gentile believers (Galatians 2:3–5). Titus had also worked with the Corinthian church and been found faithful in dealing with financial matters (2 Corinthians 8:6).

Titus was trusted by Paul to lead the churches in Crete and to straighten out the affairs there on his behalf. The trust Paul imparts in this letter implies a sincere relationship and understanding between the two men. It also implies a clarity of understanding as to what constituted the foundations of the gospel and what was clearly false teaching. Clarity on both points would be needed in order for Titus to succeed in Crete.

Much of the content of Titus refers to behaviour. The text describes what is expected of Christians in different positions in society, both in terms of their personal interactions and interactions within the groups they represent.

It can come across as a list of authoritarian instructions. However, Paul was writing to a population that had a reputation for being lazy and tending to enjoy their fallen natures a bit too much (Titus 1:12). He hoped that Titus could lift the Cretans, and in particular the Cretan church, from the moral quagmire they had been languishing in to aspire to celebrate their new life with Christ. In order that this might happen, Paul saw the need to delineate the standards that were expected as natural extensions of the people's new faith.

Of course, we are not lazy gluttons, liars, or evil brutes. We are, however, fallen individuals who have been given hope through our belief in Christ. We still have some memories of our old ways of living, and in this we have something in common with the Cretans. Titus was tasked with leading the Cretans away from those old practices and into a new life that embraced the call to be sound in the faith.

In our reading of the letter, let us neither presume that we are innocent of all the lowly behaviours listed nor that we have attained all that Paul longed for in his readers. We would do well to hold on to the truth that although our salvation is secured, we have a lifetime to work on our sanctification. Let us reflect on a word or two from this letter to see if we cannot make progress in this regard.

> If you would follow on to know the Lord, come at once to the open Bible, expecting it to speak to you. Do not come with the notion that it is a thing which you may push around at your convenience. It is more than a thing; it is a voice, a word, the very Word of the living God.[7]

—A.W. Tozer

7 Tozer, *The Pursuit of God*, 78.

Knowledge of the Truth

TITUS 1:1–4

Paul, a servant of God and an apostle of Jesus Christ to further the faith of God's elect and their knowledge of the truth that leads to godliness—[2] in the hope of eternal life, which God, who does not lie, promised before the beginning of time, [3] and which now at his appointed season he has brought to light through the preaching entrusted to me by the command of God our Savior,

[4] To Titus, my true son in our common faith: grace and peace from God the Father and Christ Jesus our Savior.

Titus was a personal letter of instruction meant to assist a young pastor establish a framework for the churches of Crete. It was a distillation of wisdom that would enable the easier selection of leaders to assist Titus in making decisions. Titus had a difficult task ahead of him and the letter was an attempt to simplify matters and enable him to succeed.

To provide some background to the instructions he was about to give, Paul begins with an introduction in this passage. He identifies his role, which is to *"further... knowledge of the truth that leads to godliness."* In essence, there is a spontaneity of behaviour that results from knowing God. Godly behaviour can be as natural as a reflex born from experiencing God.

The Greek word for knowledge used here, *epignosis*, is a composite of *gnosis* ("to know") and *epi* ("intensification") The words of 2 Timothy 1:12 come to mind as we imagine Paul writing of his experience of Christ: *"I know whom I have believed…"* There is therefore a familiarity with the truth that produces godly behaviour.

We can substitute the word truth for familiarity with God, since this is the notion behind the word as used in today's passage. The Greek word for truth, *aletheia*, speaks to its reality. For Paul, Jesus was real; he was *aletheia*. Such was his intimacy with Jesus that Paul held Him as truth, and his knowledge of Christ propelled him to godliness.

It is important to understand this in light of this letter being full of lists and potential comparisons. We will need to look beyond the inventory of characteristics we are going to find if we are to perceive that Paul is encouraging Titus to look for enlightened lives, ones that have been genuinely touched by God's grace. Titus was to look for people for whom Christ was real, lives in which the truth of Christ had had an impact.

Comparisons have been made between the letters to Philemon and the letter to Titus. The lists in Titus are, at first glance, contrary to the liberty we read of in the letter to Philemon. Paul empowered Philemon to deal with the return of Onesimus in whatever manner he saw fit. There were no imperatives, no commands, and no lists. Paul was permissive, which we appreciated as a measure of Paul's love for Philemon and a measure of Paul's respect for his fellow Christian.

In contrast, in Titus we are going to read of commands, of checklists which can be used to choose Christian leaders, as well as learn how to spot false teachers and determine how Christians should conduct themselves. By identifying a framework for behaviour and character, the letter to Titus loses some of the spontaneity we found in the note to Philemon.

Although the two letters may appear to be at odds, marrying them into a unified understanding of the Christian faith is important, otherwise one or the other may contract our own positions on pastoral matters. Are we a list or liberty person, or can we be both?

Henri Nouwen has written a helpful book in this regard about his meditations on Rembrandt's famous painting, "The Return of the Prodigal Son." In this book, he oscillates back and forth in discussing the younger prodigal son and the elder son. Nouwen identifies with both sons and sees himself in the reformed life of the reckless younger one, who leaves and returns, as well as in the duplicity of the elder brother, who is angry yet becomes reconciled by the father.

Onesimus was great example of the prodigal son, whereas the Cretans could be an example of the reconciled elder son. Both can exist in the same family and accept each other as children of the father. By extension, the libertarian philosophy of the letter to Philemon and the rigidity of the lists in Titus can co-exist within the Christian faith. However, their inclusion will stretch our understanding.

When we meet lists, like those we find in the letter to Titus, our tendency is to make comparisons. We compare the checklists to our own characteristics. As a result, we judge. This response is the result of our fallen nature through which we question our value. There is a danger, though, that in comparing ourselves to the characteristics written in the lists we will become like the elder brother, whose initial response was anger and resentment. When we make comparisons, we, like him, reflect on our dutiful service and resent the implication of the lists.

One of our challenges as we read Titus will be to extend our faith and understanding away from an angry elder brother type of response. The implication of Paul's opening lines is that we have to experience God in order for godly behaviour to manifest in our lives.

Nouwen agrees, writing that a knowledge of Christ will encourage us "to enter into his (God's) light and discover there that in God, all people are uniquely and completely loved."[8]

At the outset of the letter, Paul writes that genuine faith produces godly behaviour. He invites Titus to adopt the behaviours he saw in his father in the faith. There is an invitation here for us, too, to step into the light of God's truth and receive His embrace and blessing.

APPLICATION: KNOWLEDGE OF THE TRUTH

- Spend a moment reflecting on your own experience of God. Allow His grace to penetrate your heart

8 Henri J.M. Nouwen, *The Return of the Prodigal Son* (New York, NY: Doubleday, 1994), 81.

and allow His warmth and acceptance to bring spontaneity to your godliness.

- If you have chance, look up Rembrandt's "The Return of the Prodigal Son" painting. Reflect on how you perceive yourself. Is it the humbled prodigal son who accepts the father's embrace, or is it the proud elder brother, half in shadow and half in light, caught between the father's love and his own pride?
- Pray that as you read through Titus, you would focus on knowing Christ so that you may find godliness a natural response, as opposed to a forced duty.

Look first for grace. Do not esteem good people on account of their foibles or deficiencies in matters of little importance. Gold unpolished is far more valuable that the brightest brass. Never form unfavourable opinions of religious people hastily: charity hopeth all things.[9]

—Legh Richmond

9 Legh Richmond, *The Rev. Legh Richmond's Letters and Counsels to His Children* (Minneapolis, MN: Curiosmith, 2016), 22.

God's Stewards

TITUS 1:5–9

The reason I left you in Crete was that you might put in order what was left unfinished and appoint elders in every town, as I directed you. [6] An elder must be blameless, faithful to his wife, a man whose children believe and are not open to the charge of being wild and disobedient. [7] Since an overseer manages God's household, he must be blameless—not overbearing, not quick-tempered, not given to drunkenness, not violent, not pursuing dishonest gain. [8] Rather, he must be hospitable, one who loves what is good, who is self-controlled, upright, holy and disciplined. [9] He must hold firmly to the trustworthy message as it has been taught, so that he can encourage others by sound doctrine and refute those who oppose it.

Paul was keen to describe to Titus the types of leaders that would build community. He also wanted it understood that these individuals should appreciate who it was they were building for: God's household, which they were establishing (Titus 1:7).

This perspective is important. Once we focus on His glory, blessing, and grace, we develop a viewpoint that reflects His light, rather than seeing only our own point of view.

Read through today's passage again in light of the fact that Titus was looking for authentic individuals who weren't in church for their personal gain but for Him and His glory.

The Greek word which has been translated as "manages God's household"[10] is *oikonomos*, a composite of *oikos* ("house") and *nemo* ("manage"). In the culture of the day, an *oikonomos* might have been a slave who could be trusted to run the affairs of the household. They were also known as housekeepers or housewives. The picture is one of a dedicated individual who placed the management and smooth running of the home above their own aspirations.

If we were to try making a list of attributes that we would hope to find in a community builder, someone who would inspire and be aspired to, I suspect the list would be similar to the one given to Titus. We too would look for a mature person who has a stable family life that demonstrates faithfulness to others, someone of sobriety and of sober judgement, and a friendly and sociable type who is happy in other people's company. Most importantly, such a leader, to be an effective Christian shepherd, would have to have clear vision of the gospel.

When Titus was written, the first generation of disciples was being called home, so holding firm to a trustworthy message (Titus 1:9) was going to be vital for the church stewards in Crete. If the early church lost sight of the purity of the gospel, there was a chance it would be lost or that subsequent generations would be led astray.

When church politics were divisive, Paul had a habit of returning to the centrality of Christ. For Paul, it was never Christ

---

10 In the English Standard Version, this is translated as "God's steward."

plus additional factors; it was always the simplicity of the gospel, since Christ's life was all-sufficient. If we try to add to His gift, we diminish the gift. We are to accept the gift of His life just as it was given, without additional trimmings or provisos.

The word trustworthy (*pistos*) could also mean faithful, and the use of this word was surely accurate, for His message of salvation was and is worthy of our faith.

If any characteristics included in this list seem awkward to a modern reader, remember the trustworthy message. The critical component of our faith is that we hold fast to Christ rather than try to adhere to the list. If we remain in Him, His light will leave our concerns in the shade.

With this perspective—planted, rooted, and growing in Him—we will be better positioned to help build community in our churches and be the house stewards we have been called to be.

APPLICATION: GOD'S STEWARDS

- Reflect on the thought that as Christians we are to serve our Father in heaven.
- Consider the roles you can take on to build community within your church. Would you allow Titus to call on your assistance?
- Try and put into your own words what the trustworthy message is. An understanding of the salient points of the gospel will enable you to encourage others (Titus 1:9).

Theology itself, important as its themes and communications, sinks into mere science or literary attainments, unless founded upon, and accompanied by a devotional and affectionate application of its principles to the soul. It is much easier to be a divine that an Christian, - an eccelesiastic, than a pastor.[11]

—Legh Richmond

---

11 Legh Richmond, *Domestic Portraiture and Tracts, Seventh Edition* (New York, NY: Protestant Episcopal Society, 1859), 192.

Pure

For there are many rebellious people, full of meaning-less talk and deception, especially those of the circum-cision group. [11] They must be silenced, because they are disrupting whole households by teaching things they ought not to teach—and that for the sake of dishonest gain. [12] One of Crete's own prophets has said it: "Cretans are always liars, evil brutes, lazy gluttons." [13] This saying is true. Therefore rebuke them sharply, so that they will be sound in the faith [14] and will pay no attention to Jewish myths or to the merely human commands of those who reject the truth. [15] To the pure, all things are pure, but to those who are corrupted and do not believe, nothing is pure. In fact, both their minds and consciences are cor-rupted. [16] They claim to know God, but by their actions they deny him. They are detestable, disobedient and un-fit for doing anything good.

Paul contrasts those who are pure with those who are not. His description of the impure covers their character traits, behaviours, and attitude toward the gospel. His summary in Titus 1:16 is unceremonious and dismissive. In his search for church leaders, Titus is to ignore such people; instead he is to search out the pure, the uncorrupted, and those with minds and consciences consistent with the new life to which they have been called.

When we consider the word "pure," we picture something untainted and unsoiled, like freshly fallen white snow or clear water. In a person, we often use this word to describe someone with sincere motives, without a hidden agenda. We might think of such an individual as naive and childlike in their innocence.

The Greek word is *katharos*, from which we derive words such as catharsis or cathartic. We might use them respectively to describe emotional cleansing or an exercise to relieve stress.

Note that Paul isn't asking for newly converted Christians who might be considered washed clean. Rather, Titus is to look for mature leaders or elders. Yet how can a mature leader have childlike purity? The answer is in the difference between childlikeness and childishness. In maturity, child like faith and trust are maintained but childish behaviours, tempers, outbursts and selfishness are lost.

Paul is speaking of the need in the Cretan church for mature childlike leaders who had progressed from a newfound childish belief.

Picture a stream of pure water, which has become pure through the settling of sediment over time, or a pure pink rose which has had its genetic flaws bred out over time. The concept of purity speaks of a refining process that brings an individual to maturity.

As a Christian, purity or maturity might be perceived in multiple ways, such as dutifully passing through the rites of christening, baptism, or confirmation. Or it might be perceived by serving religiously on church rotas or being dedicated in attending church meetings.

However, I think Paul is suggesting here that *katharos* individuals are those who have a heart for God and a genuine desire to grow into maturity as father-like figures in the churches where they worship. Such individuals are pure. Their motives aren't self-seeking but rather Kingdom-seeking. Their vision is like that of their Father in heaven. They seek to forgive, be compassionate, and find joy in those they shepherd. Such individuals aren't satisfied with childish things. They aren't interested in worldly goals or myths.

These are the type of people Jesus wrote about in the Beatitudes (Matthew 5:3–12). Such individuals are hard to find. They are epitomized by their otherworldliness, which can be difficult to fathom, for their perspectives stretch and challenge ours. They aren't easily influenced by the opinions of others and are able to seek His will. They are governed not by popularist pressure but by Godly wisdom.

It was for the likes of these that Titus was to search: *"Blessed are the pure in heart, for they will see God"* (Matthew 5:8).

APPLICATION: PURE

- Consider where you are on your spiritual course. Are there aspects of your life that you are holding on to? Is there sediment that you agitate to avoid being pure?

Pure: Titus 1:10-16

- Reminisce again on the story of the prodigal son. Nouwen was surprised by the conclusion he drew from his meditations; he realized that our time is often spent considering how like the sons we are when we should rather ask whether we have become like the father. Think about this perspective. It's not enough to travel home. Our calling is to be a compassionate, spiritual parent in our homes and churches.
- Dwell on the concept of purity, meaning maturity. Pray that God would help your progress toward spiritual maturity so you can put away the childish things that prevent you from seeing Him.

Sparkle

TITUS 2:1–10

You, however, must teach what is appropriate to sound doctrine. [2] Teach the older men to be temperate, worthy of respect, self-controlled, and sound in faith, in love and in endurance.

[3] Likewise, teach the older women to be reverent in the way they live, not to be slanderers or addicted to much wine, but to teach what is good. [4] Then they can urge the younger women to love their husbands and children, [5] to be self-controlled and pure, to be busy at home, to be kind, and to be subject to their husbands, so that no one will malign the word of God.

[6] Similarly, encourage the young men to be self-controlled. [7] In everything set them an example by doing what is good. In your teaching show integrity, seriousness [8] and soundness of speech that cannot be condemned, so that those who oppose you may be ashamed because they have nothing bad to say about us.

[9] Teach slaves to be subject to their masters in everything, to try to please them, not to talk back to them, [10] and not to steal from them, but to show that

they can be fully trusted, so that in every way they will make the teaching about God our Savior attractive.

I can imagine Titus reading over these words from Paul and thinking about each of the groups Paul has addressed. As Titus brought reformation and order to the Cretan churches, he was to encourage every segment of the church community, old and young, male and female, slave and free, to step into their Christian maturity by demonstrating certain attitudes and behaviours. The emphasis of this passage was not on the individual social graces mentioned but the overall demeanour of a Christian.

Titus 2:5, 8, and 10 highlight why a Christian's disposition is so important: it directly reflects on their life philosophy, which directly reflects on the gospel. As a consequence, our home life must not provide any excuse for the word of God to be maligned (Titus 2:5). Our speech and conduct must not provide any reason for others to speak ill of us (Titus 2:8). Finally, although Titus 2:10 was directed toward slaves, we too are called to be worthy of the trust of others so that the gospel will be seen as attractive.

Sometimes in a passage like this we gloss over the parts that don't directly address our peer group. We ignore the sentiments expressed concerning others and focus only on those pertaining to ourselves. If we do this, we might ignore the overall message.

We can also misinterpret the application of the passage to our culture and our time. This might be especially relevant in the above comments regarding young women and slaves. Many godly young Christian women not only do everything that Paul mentions, they also hold down a necessary and fulfilling job. In modern life, the emphasis for young women is the same as it has always been—and that is to do all these different tasks in a manner which glorifies Christ.

Applying the final paragraph pertaining to slaves is challenging since we are not slaves and the practice of slavery has all but disappeared from civilized societies. In the final two verses, though, Paul switches from using a double negative to encourage our good behaviour—*"no one will malign"* (Titus 2:5) *"nothing bad"* (Titus 2:8)—to describing a beautiful image to help Titus motivate the Cretans. He writes that good behaviour is like a jewel in a crown and draws positive attention to the gospel.

In Titus 2:10, Paul uses the word *kosmeo*, which comes from the Greek *kosmos*, meaning adornment, decoration, or ornament. This is where we have derived the English word "cosmetic." The New International Version translates this as "attractive," thus missing some of the verse's meaning that is brought out in other translations:

> … so that in everything they may be an ornament and do credit to the teaching [which is] from and about God our Savior. (Titus 2:10, AMPCE)

> Then their good character will shine through their actions, adding luster to the teaching of our Savior God. (Titus 2:10, MSG)

Although this instruction was directed toward slaves, for me it's about the positive image Paul was trying to communicate in Titus 2:5 and 8. It offers an appealing portrait of what mature Christian behaviour looks like and stands for.

We are adorned with a priceless gift of life from Christ. It sits comfortably on our heads, and the jewels of the crown—our behaviour—draw attention to Him and His generous gift.

We are to follow the urging of Paul to behave and carry ourselves with dignity as Christians both in recognition of the blessing we were given by grace and in response to the call to shine like jewels. We are at best jewels in His crown, yet it is His will that we sparkle so that His crown will be more attractive to others.

APPLICATION: SPARKLE

- With all the instruction, urging, and teaching of rules, we can forget the fact that our behaviour or fruit, if we remain in Him, will be generous and sparkle. Thank God for His crown and pray that the image of a jewel in that crown would be an encouragement for us to follow godly patterns of behaviour.
- Consider other Christians who wear the crown of Christ and thank God for the jewels which we recognize as examples of godly behaviour in their lives.
- Quietly reflect on whether there are some jewels in your crown that need further polish to enable them to sparkle for Christ.

Eager

TITUS 2:11–15

For the grace of God has appeared that offers salvation to all people. [12] It teaches us to say "No" to ungodliness and worldly passions, and to live self-controlled, upright and godly lives in this present age, [13] while we wait for the blessed hope—the appearing of the glory of our great God and Savior, Jesus Christ, [14] who gave himself for us to redeem us from all wickedness and to purify for himself a people that are his very own, eager to do what is good.

[15] These, then, are the things you should teach. Encourage and rebuke with all authority. Do not let anyone despise you.

As mature Christians, it can be challenging to remember our origins. We have a tendency to neglect our beginnings. We overlook where we were spiritually before we encountered the grace of God.

Paul was acutely aware of his former life as a Pharisee. I suspect that not a day went by when he didn't pause to remember what kind of a person he had been.

He had committed dreadful atrocities against the church as a younger man. He had persecuted the church with zeal, believing with his whole heart that he was doing the right thing. The grace of God had appeared to him, however, and offered him salvation. Even in his depraved former life, in his role as a persecutor of the early Church and perpetrator of martyrdom, he was offered redemption.

Despite the baseness of his spiritual standing, Paul was offered a fresh beginning and clean slate. How he must have marvelled at the generosity of God's forgiveness and at the generosity of His grace to extend such acceptance.

I suspect we overlook the truth that we were, before we accepted God's grace, not much different to Paul, spiritually speaking. We too were guilty of misappropriating God's word and misinterpreting His signs (Romans 1:19–20). We too may not have been kind or forgiving to others. We may even have despised church types.

Perhaps we may feel that, although we were not perfect, we were certainly better people than Paul, who had approved of some terrible things. This attitude, although justifiable from a secular perspective, isn't accurate from a heavenly point of view. Not only is this mindset spiritually inaccurate, it's unhelpful in bringing about the maturity that God requires (Galatians 6:4–6). When we compare ourselves to others to achieve our sense of righteousness, we do Christ a disservice and fail to respect the magnitude of grace we have been given.

In these verses, Paul completes his recommendations to Titus on what ought to be taught, and in doing so he reminds

Titus that the grace of God is available to all, and that it empowers Christians to live changed lives—lives that are typified by an eagerness to do what is good (Titus 2:14).

The word eager is translated from the Greek *zelotes*, and it might also be translated as zealous. In Greek, the word is derived from *zeo*, which was used to describe something that was boiling or glowing hot. We might imagine this term to describe an individual who had reached a fever pitch over an issue, such was the strength of their passion and emotion.

This raises an interesting question, when we consider our own passion for doing good deeds or pursuing godly lives. What is it that diminishes our fervour for doing good? Why do we become lacklustre in our pursuit of holiness?

Jerry Bridges, in his book *The Pursuit of Holiness*, identifies one reason for our failure in this area. He writes that it occurs since "our attitude toward sin is more self-centred than God-centred."[12] He goes on to explain that when we search for victories over sin, we place the victory over a relationship with God.[13]

It follows that we ought to work on our relationship with God and hold this central to our lives. If we do this, the concept goes, we will be eager to do good and refrain from unholy living.

I wonder therefore if our lack of focus on God reflects our lack of appreciation for God's grace. If we understood more of what we have been given, or from where we have been rescued, we might be more attentive to God's wishes for our lives.

---

12 Jerry Bridges, *The Pursuit of Holiness* (Buckinghamshire, UK: NavPress, 1985), 21.
13 Ibid., 20.

Eager: Titus 2:11-15

Paul's interaction with Christ had a profound effect in his life. He recentred his zeal away from persecution to pursuit of Christ.

I suspect that our own perspectives would be altered by taking a moment or two to refocus our thoughts away from our perceived righteousness to His grace. Gaining a new appreciation of his grace (Titus 2:11) would have a similar effect as it did to Paul, and we would feel eager to do what is good.

APPLICATION: EAGER

- Reflect for a moment on the grace that has been bestowed on you to bring you from a spiritual wilderness to becoming a child of God.
- How do you wish to respond to that gift of grace? Does it make you eager to do good and live a life befitting of the grace you have been afforded?
- Consider how reflecting on God's grace can lead you to recentre your perspective. Pray that this renewed focus on God and His generosity might reform any ungodly pursuits in you so that, like Paul, any zeal in your life will be directed toward doing good.

Washing

Remind the people to be subject to rulers and
authorities, to be obedient, to be ready to do whatever
is good, [2] to slander no one, to be peaceable and
considerate, and always to be gentle toward everyone.

[3] At one time we too were foolish, disobedient,
deceived and enslaved by all kinds of passions and
pleasures. We lived in malice and envy, being hated and
hating one another. [4] But when the kindness and love
of God our Savior appeared, [5] he saved us, not because
of righteous things we had done, but because of his
mercy. He saved us through the washing of rebirth
and renewal by the Holy Spirit, [6] whom he poured
out on us generously through Jesus Christ our Savior,
[7] so that, having been justified by his grace, we might
become heirs having the hope of eternal life. [8] This is
a trustworthy saying. And I want you to stress these
things, so that those who have trusted in God may be
careful to devote themselves to doing what is good.
These things are excellent and profitable for everyone.

[9] But avoid foolish controversies and genealogies
and arguments and quarrels about the law, because

these are unprofitable and useless. [10] Warn a divisive person once, and then warn them a second time. After that, have nothing to do with them. [11] You may be sure that such people are warped and sinful; they are self-condemned.

As Paul begins to close out his letter to Titus, he has some final instructions for his prodigy. Some of these are personal and others are corporate, to be given to the church.

Paul's words of encouragement would have been important for Titus as he sought to lead reform and realign the Cretan church. To be successful in his task, Titus would have needed a sustainable purpose, perpetual optimism, and reliable conflict resolution tools. Without these, he would have made little progress and may have gotten bogged down in the first town he visited as he sought to straighten out fractious church politics and deal with interpersonal conflicts.

In this passage, we see Paul deliberately writing personally to Titus, reminding him of God's grace, but doing so in such a way that doesn't let us miss the sense of renewal that is ours in Christ (Titus 3:5).

Paul speaks of our renewal through washing, a reference to the ceremonial baptism which is part of our declaration of faith. This represents a ceremonial and figurative wash, cleaning us from our old lives as we enter the new life of a Christian. It also speaks to the constant rewashing and renewal that is touched on by Paul in 2 Corinthians. We are renewed daily:

Therefore we do not lose heart. Though outwardly we are wasting away, yet inwardly we are being renewed day by day. For our light and momentary troubles are achieving for us an eternal glory that far outweighs them all. So we fix our eyes not on what is seen, but on what is unseen, since what is seen is temporary, but what is unseen is eternal. (2 Corinthians 4:16–18)

There are two Greek words which can be used for the act of washing someone or something clean. One is the verb *nipto* and was used to describe washing specific items, such as dipping your feet in water. A different word is used in Titus 3:5, *loutron*, a noun which refers to whole-body cleansing or bathing.

Paul makes the point that we are continually made clean by the saving grace of Christ. Ours is not a *nipto* cleaning, but a *loutron* regeneration. We have been made sparkling clean, to use the analogy of a prior chapter. Titus is reassured that he has been completely recleaned on a daily basis, which would have been important as he faced opposition and conflict from the church. Without the sense of this regeneration through the beautiful gift of cleansing, no doubt he would have become overwhelmed in the dusty works of dealing with sinful churches.

Our missions may not be as extensive as that of Titus, but we are on a mission as Christians—at home, in our workplaces, and when we play at our hobbies. We will encounter dusty roads and experience conflict. This can ruin our sense of harmony with one another and with God. Our conflicts tend to destabilize the peace which our relationship with Christ brings, making us cling to hurts and sour our interactions with others.

In these verses, Paul reminds Titus and ourselves of the importance of our total cleansing by grace—and he tells us not to dwell on conflicts (Titus 3:9–10). Although I find the first part of Paul's instructions uplifting and refreshing, I find that the second part takes tremendous faith. I often want to dwell in the conflict to see if I can sort it out myself rather than leave it with God.

This is a natural response, I suspect, one that speaks to our independence and perhaps arrogance. However, this response has no place in our lives if we are truly motivated and promoted by God's love. Paul would suggest, or perhaps insist, that we "let go and let God":

> Now to him who is able to do immeasurably more than all we ask or imagine, according to his power that is at work within us, to him be glory in the church and in Christ Jesus throughout all generations, for ever and ever! Amen. (Ephesians 3:20–21)

I find it reassuring that a mature Christian like Titus needed to be reminded of these things. It makes me appreciate that it would be good for me to consider these disciplines in my own life. In challenging circumstances, we need to dwell on both aspects: the refreshing cleanse of His saving grace and a reliance on His wisdom rather than our independence.

APPLICATION: WASHING

- Consider the difference you feel when you compare the act of washing just your face versus taking a shower. We are refreshed through the grace of Christ, not just partially but completely, and this is a daily occurrence. Thank Jesus for your complete cleansing by His grace.
- The renewal we feel when we acknowledge being saved by His grace should relegate any conflicts in our lives to the shadows. Ask for God's strength to keep them in the shadows by relying on His might rather than your own.
- Thank God for the courage of Titus to work amongst the Cretans. His was a challenging ministry and one that should inspire our own.

Help on Their Way

TITUS 3:12–15

As soon as I send Artemas or Tychicus to you, do your best to come to me at Nicopolis, because I have decided to winter there. [13] Do everything you can to help Zenas the lawyer and Apollos on their way and see that they have everything they need. [14] Our people must learn to devote themselves to doing what is good, in order to provide for urgent needs and not live unproductive lives.

[15] Everyone with me sends you greetings. Greet those who love us in the faith. Grace be with you all.

Titus wasn't left alone on Crete to reform the church there. He appears to have had support from a lawyer (or scribe) named Zenas and from Apollos, who we know as a gifted teacher and evangelist (Acts and 1 Corinthians).

Nor was Titus left with an unending role. Paul saw to it that Artemas and Tychicus would relieve him of his duties. Knowing that we have a window of time in which to complete difficult tasks focusses the mind and our work. Whether this was Paul's motive or whether he was just looking forward to having Titus close by over the winter, we cannot be sure, yet it was wise personnel management.

Titus had no time to grow stale in his detachment in Crete nor could he dillydally if he were to complete his assignment.

Paul must have marvelled at times as he reflected on the resources God had provided. Including Titus, here were five converts to Christianity—converts who had been so convinced of the truth and value of the gospel that they had adopted a nomadic existence to continue spreading the word and build the early church throughout the Mediterranean basin. They were apparently intelligent men, educated and capable, implying that they had abandoned much to take up this new way of life.

It is worth pausing on this to thank God for His provision to ensure that the miracle of conversion possessed these individuals so strongly that they were willing to forgo so much for His glory.

Paul hints at the difficulties faced by the travellers in Titus 3:13. Here, he asks that Titus do everything he can to help Zenas and Apollos on their way. The Greek verb *propempo* is translated as "help on their way."

We might think today of the notion paying it forward. In the original sense, *propempo* means providing sufficient resources to enable the beneficiary to complete their journey or task. Paul was asking for more than sufficient resources; he required that Titus be generous in his provision to provide everything they would need.

Propempo is constructed from *pro* ("before") and *pempo* ("to send"). We understand then that the wherewithal to complete the task was sent ahead of time to ensure it could be completed.

This is a rich thought on which to complete our readings in Titus, for the concept of *propempo* can be applied not just to Zenas and Apollos but to ourselves and for our fellow Christians.

This idea underlies much of the purpose of teaching, training, and ministry. Our educators in these areas aim to help us on our way and supply all that we need to complete the tasks God has in hand.

Titus had a role to fulfil in providing *propempo* for his fellow workers. I suspect that we have similar roles too. Whether they be of a spiritual dimension through prayer ministry or involve practical logistic help, there are ways we can pay it forward.

Christ achieved the greatest *propempo* through His death on the cross. Our way to the Father has been graciously resourced through His sacrifice. Our journey through this life into the next has been made possible by Him. It is not something we could have accomplished on our own.

In following His lead in our lives, our motivation is not that we hope to repay His *propempo*, for it would be folly for us to try to repay Jesus, just as it would be foolish for an ancient traveller to attempt to repay his sponsor.

Our motivation for following His lead is to mirror the grace we have been extended. An appropriate response is to be so affected by the generosity of His *propempo*, His grace, that we, like Titus, Artemas, Tychicus, Zemas, and Apollos, desire to live for Him and not ourselves.

APPLICATION: HELP ON THEIR WAY

- Consider the ways in which others have resourced your walk with Christ, whether it be through discipleship, ongoing ministry, or prayer. Thank God for His and their generosity.

- Despite his busy ministry, Titus was tasked with ensuring that Apollos and Zenas were provided for. Pray that you would not be so fatigued by your own ministries that you would be unable to provide for others in theirs.
- Look for opportunities to pay it forward today—not just financially, but with kind words, a prayer, or other means. May God bless you richly for your acts of grace.

Reflections

TITUS

> The reason I left you in Crete was that you might put in order what was left unfinished and appoint elders in every town, as I directed you. (Titus 1:5)

The bookmark I used during my readings in Titus was a postcard depicting Dunnottar Castle in Scotland. It was a formidable castle in its heyday, infamous for the internment of Christian covenanters and famous for its strong defences since it is encircled on three sides by the fearsome North Sea.

I had no particular reason for choosing this postcard. I suspect it was just on hand when I began my studies.

However, when I now reflect on the lessons from Paul's letter to Titus, the castle reminds me of some of the demands made on our Christian character during our lifetimes. We are called to have purpose and strong foundations in our faithful walk. We are called to take our stand against the winds of change and waves of pressure to conform to the patterns of this modern time.

Prior to the visit of Paul and Titus, the Cretan church was struggling to take its stand. Even as Paul left, there were issues to straighten out. Drawing together the themes of Titus, it seems apparent that Paul's letter to Titus was a call to maturity on many levels.

In leaving his disciple in charge, Paul was summoning Titus to assume a position of seniority, to be a leader and demonstrate Christian maturity. Titus in turn was to call upon the Cretan church as a corporate body to become mature in their practices. His message was for them to throw off signs of immaturity and rebellion and choose to conduct themselves in ways that were befitting of their new lives in Christ. Titus was to look for maturity in church members and to select those who demonstrated Christian seasoning for positions of authority and leadership.

Assuming a position of maturity isn't easy. The challenges of leadership don't disappear with the passage of time.

Dunnottar Castle still bears the brunt of the North Sea's winds and storms, yet it stands. It stands because of its firm footing on an unusual rock foundation. For our faith to stand, it will need to built on the foundation of Christ. His is a foundation of grace which serves to reinforce our footing and enables us to stand firm.

We, like the Cretans, can become stale in our appreciation of grace. Just as I stopped appreciating the view of the castle on my postcard, we too can become so accustomed to talking of God's grace that we fail to fully recognize and value its true significance.

Could it be that a person's lack of maturity is due to an incomplete grasp of the enormity of God's grace? Paul wrote of God's grace four times in his letter to Titus: once before beginning his list of imperatives (Titus 1:4), twice after making controversial points (Titus 2:7, 11) and then again in his closing statements.

Grace is such an unhuman quality that we need to be reminded of it if we are going to mature in our faith. Grace is an unnatural response when we experience hurt or insult, or when folks disagree with us. However, this is what Christian maturity looks like: we respond with grace and don't react with a reflex.

Grace does not mean we crumble. Dunnottar Castle is still standing firm upon its rock. We too must stand, but this can be done by avoiding foolish arguments, being obedient to authorities, being peaceable, and showing humility.

Paul left Titus to straighten things out and finish that which had been left unfinished. Christ has left us, too, but we are not orphans and not without support; we are to finish that which has been left unfinished in spreading the gospel and encouraging others to reach for Christian maturity.

Acts 20:28–35 tells of Paul's departing words to the Ephesian church. This message is relevant, for it indicates what he believed were important duties for elders and pastors. Acts 20:32 in particular reveals that our motive as Christians in whatever sphere of ministry we find ourselves—whether at home, in our families, at work, or in church—is God's grace, for it is His grace upon which we build our castles now and in eternity.

> Now I commit you to God and to the word of his grace, which can build you up and give you an inheritance among all those who are sanctified. (Acts 20:32)

When we face the storms, conflicts, and difficult choices as Titus did, let us remember that we stand firmly on His grace, not on our own strength or righteousness. If our motives are pure and driven by our response to His grace, that very same grace will enable us to respond in maturity. Only by being mature in our faith will we be effective in our commission.

If the letter to Titus is a lesson for us on the balance of maturity and grace, I hope that our readings in this devotional have seasoned our faith to become better established and more appreciative of God's gift. Spending time in the Bible seems to have this effect.

When we step away from our readings into everyday life, however, we will hopefully work with intention on the lesson and take with us some of our newfound maturity so we can finish that which has been left unfinished.

For Further Reading

David E. Garland, *Colossians/Philemon: NIV Application Commentary* (Grand Rapids, MI: Zondervan, 1998).

Walter L. Liefeld, *1 & 2 Timothy/Titus: NIV Application Commentary* (Grand Rapids, MI: Zondervan, 1998).

William Barclay, *The Letters to Timothy, Titus, and Philemon: The New Daily Study Bible* (Louisville, KY: Westminster John Knox Press, 2003).

Martin Luther King, Jr., *The Autobiography of Martin Luther King, Jr.,* ed. Clayborne Carson (New York, NY: Intellectual Properties Management Inc., Grand Central Publishing, 2001).

The Greek translations in this book have been paraphrased from material found at: "Verse by Verse Commentary by Book," *Precept Austin.* Date of access: August 3, 2022 (www.preceptaustin.org/verse_by_verse).

Proceeds from the sales of this book will be donated to St. Timothy's Christian Classical Academy, Ottawa and LOCAL Church, Ottawa.

ST. TIMOTHY'S CHRISTIAN CLASSICAL ACADEMY, OTTAWA

St. Timothy's is a small interdenominational Christian school for seventy to eighty pupils from Senior Kindergarten to Grade Eight. It was founded by a group of families in 2005 and has grown to its current size over the past eighteen years. It is a charitable organization and seeks to offer classical education in a Christian environment to children from a broad range of backgrounds. This is achieved through generous provision of tuition assistance.

The dedicated faculty at St Timothy's seek to lead their students to revere truth, desire goodness, and rejoice in beauty. The school has been housed in several locations throughout Ottawa since its inception but would ideally seek to establish a home for itself.

In the meantime, the school continues to be a beacon for Christ in the inner city. St. Timothy's strives to bless children, parents, and broader community so as to fulfill the ambassadorial role that Paul strove for in his pupil Timothy.

Further details can be found online: www.st-timothys.ca

LOCAL CHURCH, OTTAWA

LOCAL Church is spread over four campuses across southern Ontario—in Kingston, Ottawa, Toronto, and online. It is a young church and was founded by pastors Levi and Nadia Marychurch, who emigrated from New Zealand to Canada in 2018.

LOCAL Church seeks to foster a community feel in whichever campus one attends. The congregations come from diverse backgrounds, with a significant proportion of attendees being young adults and students.

The church preaches and professes a Christ-focused message. It has generous ministries in local and international charitable giving. LOCAL vigorously promotes the benefits of small group discipleship ministry.

More details of the ministry and work of the church can be found online: www.localchurch.co

A WORD FROM HIS WORD
BY GARY R. SMALL

Each chapter of *A Word from His Word* focuses on a single word or phrase from a short biblical passage. It is the author's prayer that by returning to a simplified but effective approach to Bible reading, your daily times with God's word will be invigorated. Enjoy the entire series!

NOW AVAILABLE:

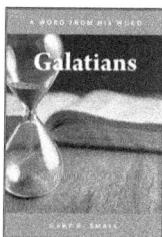

Galatians	*Colossians*
Ephesians	*1&2 Thessalonians*
Philipians	

COMING SOON:

Romans	*2 Corinthians*
1 Corinthians	*1 & 2 Timothy*